Beaches and Bays

Written by Hawys Morgan

Collins

Beaches and bays

At the beach, it is fun to play in the sand with a spade or rake.

You may see seashells, crabs and sand fleas.

scallop

sand flea

Seagulls gaze at the beach, looking for a meal.

Seagulls stay safe on the beach when there are gales and storms.

Rock pools

Heaps of seaweed sway in the rock pool.

Starfish (or sea stars) are star-shaped, but they are not fish!

starfish

sea urchin

7

Cliffs

Puffins nest on the towering cliffs. They stay on their eggs for six weeks.

Puffins' beaks transform with the seasons.
In winter, the beak fades to grey.

Rabbits graze on the green fields on top of the cliffs.

Snakes sleep in the sunlight.

This field leads to a steep cliff!

adder

Caves

Sea caves sit at the base of the cliffs.

A moray eel hurries into the shade of the cave.

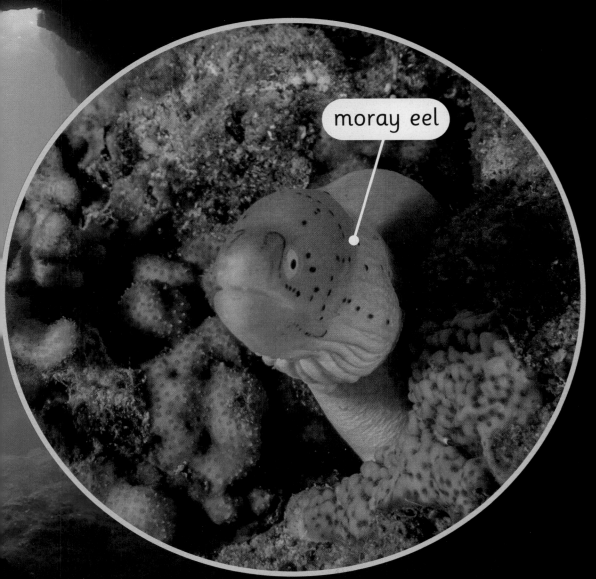

moray eel

Rocks

Grey seals sleep on the smooth rocks in the bay. They eat fish, like cod, hake and bream.

Seal pups have cream fur.

In the sea

Under the waves, rays and skates flap long fins like wings to swim.

skate

They are similar to sharks, but they are flatter in shape.

ray

Away at sea, orcas play in the clear waves.
They leap in the air.

Orcas have sharp teeth. They eat:
- fish
- seals
- sharks
- rays.

A day at the beach will amaze you!

Take away your rubbish to keep beaches and bays clean.

Beaches and bays

fields

cliffs

bay

beach

rocks

sea

23

 After reading

Letters and Sounds: Phase 5

Word count: 253

Focus phonemes: /ai/ ay, ey, a-e /ee/ ie, ea

Common exception words: be, by, you, there, like, have, your, to, the, are, their, of, when

Curriculum links: Human and physical geography

National Curriculum learning objectives: Reading/word reading: read other words of more than one syllable that contain taught GPCs; Reading/comprehension: understand both the books they can already read accurately and fluently and those they listen to by checking that the text makes sense to them as they read, and correcting inaccurate reading

Developing fluency

- Your child may enjoy hearing you read the book.
- Take turns to read a page. Read with enthusiasm and excitement to encourage your child to read with expression. Check they read the labels too.

Phonic practice

- Focus on the /ai/ and /ee/ sounds.
- Ask your child to read these words, and then identify the letter or letters that make the /ai/ sound.

  rays   graze   grey   gales   they   play

- Look together at the warning sign on page 11. Challenge your child to find three words in which the /ee/ sound is written differently. (*field, leads, steep*) Ask them to identify the letters that make the /ee/ sound. Can your child find the /ee/ sound in two words on page 6? (*heaps, seaweed*)

Extending vocabulary

- Can your child think of a synonym (word with a similar meaning) for the following?

  page 9: **transform** (e.g. *change, alter*)   page 18: **leap** (e.g. *jump, spring*)

  page 13: **hurries** (e.g. *rushes, races*)

- Reread the sentences together with your child's suggested word in place of the original. Does it make sense?